the END *of the* CLOCKWORK UNIVERSE

Books by Fleda Brown

Fishing with Blood
Do Not Peel the Birches
The Devil's Child
Breathing In, Breathing Out
The Women Who Loved Elvis All Their Lives
Reunion
Loon Cry
Driving with Dvořák
No Need of Sympathy
My Wobbly Bicycle: Meditations on Cancer and the Creative Life
The Woods Are on Fire
Growing Old in Poetry: Two Poets, Two Lives (with Sydney Lea)
Flying Through a Hole in the Storm
Mortality, with Friends
The End of the Clockwork Universe

the END *of the* CLOCKWORK UNIVERSE

Fleda Brown

Carnegie Mellon University Press
Pittsburgh 2025

Acknowledgments

The author would like to thank the editors of the following journals where these poems first appeared:

AGNI: "Catalytic Converters"
American Journal of Poetry: "Black," "All Those Dead Trees"
Catamaran: "Snapping Turtle"
The Gettysburg Review: "Sunday Morning," "This Week," "Water Bear, Phylum Tardigrada," "Ever-Fixéd Mark"
Image: "You Thought You Could Make Things Be a Certain Way"
The Kenyon Review: "Doctor of the World"
New Letters: "Ducts"
Prairie Schooner: "Photo of Two Old Men"
Quartet: "The Hooded Merganser Cure"
The Southern Review: "Remains"
Plume: "Someone Is Walking the Pig," "Something About Old Women"
The Missouri Review: "The Walk Poems, I, III, IV, VI, IX, X."

My writing group for the past fifteen years, Teresa Scollon, Catherine Turnbull, Anne Marie Oomen, Jennifer Steinorth, and Ellen Welker continue to help me in ways sometimes subtle, sometimes huge, with their fierce listening and encouragement. I'm eternally grateful to Syd Lea, the other half of our mutual admiration society. And I've brought every poem, like a cat bringing a mouse to the door, to my husband Jerry, the reader I always trust first. And it's been wonderful to work with Connie Amoroso, a gem of an editor at Carnegie Mellon University Press.

Book design by Connie Amoroso

"Prediction is very difficult, especially about the future."

—Niels Bohr

for Jerry, whose love and support makes these poems possible

CONTENTS

I

II

III

IV

V

I

"Christ! What are patterns for?"

—Amy Lowell

WILD SWEET PEA

In the margin between the hard surface and the grasses,
a tangle of small pink wings: sweet peas.

I read that the brain naturally gravitates toward negative
thoughts. A negativity bias. A wariness, a worry

for survival. Nevertheless, extravagant shades of pink.
Nevertheless, the billows of August, pointlessly excellent,

textured, wings (open hands), afloat on a sea of green
on this day in which the eye is sick from colluding with

the mind. In which there is this clarity, this brilliance,
and a gust of birds. We are all in the same place!

We (the everything of everything) are like lovers
who must ignore each other a while in order to turn

back, new, the only new possible when you've
been together forever in this life. You're willing then

to risk each other again. The small blossoming fear
that comes with knowing this will end.

WALK I

After a mile or so arthritis begins to tighten my back
    and I start trudging, walking to keep walking,
through the cattails, the soft wood of the boardwalk.
    The cattails have shed to flaky white, stalks crushed
in wide swaths. Did you know they're edible? The whole
    plant! I also talk to someone when I walk, not myself
or God. Maybe you. I imagine someone reading my thoughts
    like a book, so I'd better think something interesting.
Maybe deer bed down in the crushed stalks. But it's wet
    in there. There are recipes online for making flour
from cattail pollen. You just shake it into a bag. They say
    you can get several pounds without half trying.
There's a recipe for pollen pancakes. *Yummy!* the recipe says.
    When I tell you things you may not have known, I feel
I have at least provided something interesting.
    I cross the road where the plaque is for the Black Willow
Champion Tree of Michigan, dead of old age, its trunk
    crumbled to shreds. A Champion tree is the biggest
of its kind. I've often thought of writing a poem about it.
    The poem would say that nothing lasts, but you already
know that, so the tree goes on breaking down unsung,
    and I keep on walking with my arthritis past its fallen
tangle of branches beside the stream. I didn't mention
    the stream. Every time I walk by I think at first it's distant
traffic, until I see the gleaming from under the leaves.
    The willow muse was named for Zeus's nurse Helice,
which means willow, sacred to poets. Most things
    have a story to make them more interesting. When we
hear it, we think we've discovered their secret,
    but actually they're our stories, bouncing back at us

like a mirror, while the tree or whatever goes on being
itself. What I was thinking was like a breeze, a small
disruption, that passed down the path without a trace.

SUNDAY MORNING

"I had a dream, which was not all a dream.
The bright sun was extinguish'd, and the stars
Did wander darkling in the eternal space . . ."
—Lord Byron, "Darkness"

I
Exactly no one knows what happens
inside an atom, do they?
Electrons whiz around a tiny nucleus.
A lot of gaps in there.
No one knows how quarks work
inside the protons and neutrons, either.

II
At last we've heard gravitational waves chirping at us.
Some comfort in that. They're a little like chickadees.
A chickadee goes *chick-a-dee-dee-dee*.
They repeat the *dees* as many times as the threat seems to warrant.
They have many other sounds. *Fee-bee-bee* means *hello sweetie*.
A broken *dee* from the female to the male means *bring me a grub*.
A gurgle is a copulation sound.
If they want to keep contact with the flock, they go *tseet*.

III
The gravitational waves are going *tseet*.

IV
Birds often stand for the divine,
for what seems to wing above, like angels,
maybe going *tseet* so fast humans can't keep up.
Tweets fly through the atmosphere, messy and random.
There are rules, true, but what a horrible mess
you have to wade through: a thousand scattered

seedlings, only one or two piercing the overstory.
Bodies trapped in mines, under buildings,
raped, drowned, frozen, glaciers melting, meteors
crashing into planets, sunspots flaring out.

V

From close range, you have a raging lunatic God;
from long range, scientists chart, project, graph,
point, quantify. How would angels see all this?
Never mind, they just take orders.
They levitate enough to see quietly and tenderly
from a height, as over a newborn baby.

VI

The route through what keeps everything wound
and winding keeps on staying quiet. If you were God,
it would be necessary to let everything pass through,
the Holocaust included. You would want to be careful
not to disturb a butterfly because the shifting
might turn mountains into sand. Remember
"O Little Town of Bethlehem": "How silently,
how silently, the wond'rous gift is giv'n"?
If you break into history you better be careful.
You could end up turning the wheel
another billion years.

VII

I have never liked Sunday mornings.
They're strange, physical, like a lift in the stomach.
There's the expectation that I will lift myself
out of the mundane and enter the vague
temple of metaphor. Metaphor for what?

The feeling is like mice hiding in the walls.
Not all is seen, and the unseen is thriving
in spite of my declarations of ownership,
my documents that say this is my house.

VIII
What if the Big Bang turned around
to see itself coming? Stories that appeared to be true
would look different from there.
Let's not argue about our disparate politics.
The Gnostic split was part of it, equal and opposite forces.
You can feel the pulling, your tendency toward
the opposite, the strumming
of your vocal chords against the air.

IX
Can you turn around?
Can ancient history lose its abstraction
and turn back into stones, water,
sprites and song? Can the air turn voluptuous?
Can you see what you missed?
Wally's beloved black-and-white form
is as clear to me in the compression of time
as if he were still wanting his dinner.

X
Say any word long enough and it will vaporize.
Preachers, evangelists, have stayed on their knees until the floor's buckled.
The heavens have opened so wide they're stretched out, flaccid,
objects farther and farther apart. And what's in between?

Dust? Neutrinos? Cosmic rays? Even nuclear physicists
can't say what things *are*.
They can only say what they do, how they behave.

XI
The moment the ape saw itself, it began to climb from the floor
of the world toward the punch-drunk billiard table of the sky.
What bothers me is that you could make anything out of
the stars, the way they're arranged.

XII
A Sunday morning sensation is in me, lately, a sensation
I thought I'd gotten rid of. Not visual. It emits a light, but not visual.
My body in the same chair but projected, conflated, utterly serious.
The word awestruck might do it. And a little bit parental,
like the Magi, carrying their vials of metaphor.
I did say, though, metaphors irritate me, the way they fuse
a feeling into shapes. The way they are neither this nor that,
neither both nor neither.

CRIME NOVELS

You can almost see the slam-bang comic stars
above the female FBI agent's head. Ah-ha! Got you now!
Like when the stink bugs flew in the open window
and I swatted for days, one after the other, ridding the world
of cancer, Alzheimer's, injustice, the Great Salt Lake sinking,
with only a small weapon at my disposal. You reach a tipping point
when your brain obliterates the moral worth of stink bugs,
their right to live their armored little brown lives.
When all that matters is that you can go on unhampered
with your own life, or, rather in your own curated hamper.
On *Tiny House Nation*, Zach builds drawers under stairs,
a table that pulls out from under the sofa, a soundproof
sliding door so one can play the ukulele while the other reads,
all managed inside 225 square feet, which is a lot like
the novels I keep reading while glaciers are calving
and general political civility devolves into snarls.
Yet someone has found a way that fish-poop water can feed
cannabis and lettuce without using up our precious soil!
This is like the tiny house, getting the most with the least.
At the end of the novel, you kind of saw it coming, but not
quite the way you thought, so there was that bit of surprise.
                              Neils Bohr told Heisenberg,
walking the streets of Copenhagen arm in arm, the end
of the clockwork universe of Newton had arrived,
that nothing can be absolutely solved. If we can't know
where an electron is and how it moves, we can't predict
the exact path it takes, only multiple possible paths.
I really dislike those mysteries that allow you to choose
how it comes out. I don't want to be God, I only want
to feel a satisfying click now and then, to know the latch
is working, that some things are kept out, others in,
and FBI agents are having a beer in celebration.

THE WORST YEAR IN HUMAN HISTORY

was AD 536. Just for an example of what was lost,
it's the classic period of the Mayan civilization.
Real societies, cities, sewage systems, music scenes.

Not quite the modern world, but close. Then Halley's
Comet whipped earth with its tail. Next, volcanoes.
Yellow dust raining down like snow. A year and a half

of solid winter. The coldest decade ever. Massive
crop failures, famine. In China by the 540s,
north of the Yellow River, eight out of ten people

died. And because the crops failed, what
was there to eat but the corpses of the dead? Did
they think it was the end of the world? It wasn't.

My first husband's grandmother said the world
was ending, and I said to myself, "Selfish old lady,
doesn't want anything to go on when she's gone."

Still, the world kept slowly ending. From the moment
I was born. I can vouch for that, at least.
In Scandinavia in those ancient times they ate the rats.

The sky was dark, so no vitamin D. So in 541,
Justinian's Plague spread across Europe, killed tens
of millions of people. Birds died. The sun lost its color,

left no noontime shadows. The earth was like walking
on dried grass, the scurrying of rats' feet over the fields.
An act of the gods, surely. But now it's us, you might

say. Which is worse—the gods as heedless monsters,
throwing their oversized bodies into our affairs,
or us, puny as we are, inventing plastic and fracking?

I don't mean to be depressing. Actually, I am quite
happy. I get my basket for the farmer's market: onions,
potatoes, kale, cabbage, cheese, maple syrup,

spread out, a tenderness across the tables, beautiful
colors of carrots. Carrots like the legs of stout women!
This is when I'm alive! Two thousand and twenty plus

whatever! I am not going to waste a minute of it.
In Ethopia, hymns from that old dark era are called
"Mawaset," which means answers. Under the sound

of the mezmer, a heavy thrumming, the "zema" as if
the eardrum is vibrating poems to the body. Instead of
answers, some sort of singing, kisses into the void.

CATALYTIC CONVERTERS

Gangs are stealing catalytic converters, at night jacking up the cars just
enough, sawing off the converters with battery-powered saws.

It is the metals more precious than gold. Platinum, palladium, rhodium.
They change dirty exhaust to clean with chemical reactions.

I gave my Prius to my grandson and first thing, in Brooklyn, the c.c. was stolen.
Thieves will find the most valuable thing. They have a nose for it.

You can get that view of the world, you can stay on high alert for the faint smell
of gain. The ecosystem needs hyenas, vultures, carrion beetles

to clean up the mess. If you look at it that way, you can feel for the guy
under the car, trying to make a living, dishonest, true, but whenever

has the world been good to him? All life forms are converting to fit
the situation, to stabilize the planet. It is hard to see this up close, when

your car makes a terrible noise and the buffer between you and rotten-
egg smell is gone. It seems so unfair, because it's your car, you paid for it,

you took care of it. You try to understand, you build a story
that involves criminals and good people. You like this story because

it has energy in it, a clash of intentions. It is like a love story, two people
finding each other, embracing, only in yours there are handcuffs. Still, you've

worked toward a relationship. While in the so-called real world the villains
are out there making a killing, which is a feeling you have like free radicals

breaking down cells, protein, and DNA. You know you're growing older.
You're caught in a unified field that pulls one way and the other. Sometimes

you're the victim, sometimes the perp. This has been going on for so long you could almost fall quietly asleep as it rocks back and forth.

WALK II

The guts of the hospital spill out behind: gas lines,
    plant, the three tall smokestacks, or vents,
breath and light for those who need breath and light.
    Someone is always behind the work, working
the equipment, the Oompa-Loompas, you could say,
    but don't, because funny as the word is, they're the brown
too-slave-like dwarfs in *Charlie and the Chocolate Factory*.
    Someone is always behind the work, agreed, but let's
make them strong and willing with their sleeves rolled up
    like in the war posters. Even my walk is behind this
poem, you could say. I might have been thinking
    how I'd use the stacks and pipes. Pull them in as if
I were a street cleaner, sucking up leaves and grinding
    them into this. The workers who emerge here
are wearing scrubs and pulling off their masks as they
    take a breath of daylight. I can't seem to get past
details in my mind, nothing soaringly lyrical, just
    plodding along on the sidewalk. You don't stay on
sidewalks in a poem. You head out across a meadow,
    or dirt path, the one less traveled. I would have to
get in the car and drive to a meadow, but how
    would that look, using gas to get to the nature which
is ultimately being destroyed by gas? But there's
    the good part, the speed with which people can be
transported to the hospital, the helipad across
    the street with its bullseye and its little house to take
the stretcher in and bring it underground to the hospital.
    When the helicopter's landing, I get a little breathless
with excitement, the frantic roaring blades, the perfect
    descent like a huge dragonfly. Someday there will be
only those comparisons to nature left, while the real
    nature will be too sick to help me out here. It will need

a stretcher. The helpers are rushing in with their
     electric cars and their solar panels. It is a race against
time, as they say, the patient losing so much blood.
     Someone will be applying compression. Maybe
someone will be reciting a poem, compressing even
     language as an added remedy, in case that helps.

REMAINS

On the post office counter was a box that said cremated remains,
Priority Mail, tracked and insured. Would someone just leave it?

A body is heavy, even thus. The bones don't melt down as small
as you might think. *Remains* implies what's left after the soul.

When the funeral home said to pick up my father's remains, it felt
like an admonition, like clean up after yourself, I don't know why.

Chaff from wheat, dross from gold. Why must we always pull
things apart? If we buried the body, I think the soul could so much

more easily rest until it's ready. It could consider. It could crouch
and listen for the slightest nudge, then it could levitate through

the coffin, through the soil, upward into the pink evening when
no one is looking. I am sorry for the soul that has to fly furiously out

ahead of the flames, that has had to leave its beloved before all
has been resolved. Its beloved, waiting in the post office like a child

left in care of, wearing a tag. Waiting for someone they said would
come. Maybe the soul is still hanging on a bit, little sparks of soul

among the ashes. To think of no soul feels like stone, but even stone
has its interior channels, its compressions. How long had the box

been there? How long would you wait beside it as if it were a small
stray animal? What passes through the post office is always holding

its breath, waiting to get somewhere. It is weighing me down to think
of this. I want to think of the worms, the slow breath of oxygen. I want

the Big Bang to circle back around to the beginning, I want matter
to open its arms and take back whatever it said to cause this rift.

SOMEONE IS WALKING THE PIG

Someone is walking the pig in our downstairs hallway, where the shops are.
No, I forgot, the pig is staying home safe these days. She's a big pig,
black with a white stripe down her snout, bright pink nostrils
and hooves, as pigs have. She was wearing a pink flowered harness.
Pigs are very smart. This one made little snorts when petted.
She was an ordinary surprise in the hallway, back when things were
ordinary. Days went on with their catastrophes and sorrows
and weddings and dances. A graph of those days would reach up
to about a four or five, and below the line, about the same.
This was before the graph began to look like Mt. Everest
above, and the pit of hell below. A pig with a flowered harness
would be swallowed alive by the recent excitements.
There are about a billion pigs alive at any one time.
They can learn their names and they have excellent memories.
They like music, and they sympathize with each other
when one is in distress. They are ordinary in that way like us.
When our pig used to come here, everyone would stop
to greet her as if there were some enchantment in being a pig.
Of course it is not that long ago that there were deep
dark forests, and pigs digging truffles, and three little pigs
in their houses of straw and sticks and bricks. Now all this regret,
as if we don't know how to end a story properly anymore,
as if we've forgotten the moral and just awkwardly watch the pig
to see if it will do something clever, but not too clever.

II

"If you're lucky, she once said
elliptically and apropos of nothing
specific, *it will bring you to your knees."*

—Kate Daniels, of Gertrude Stein

WALKING IN THE SPRING GRASSES

I understand that when there's enough matter in the universe,
including dark matter, gravity will halt the expansion and begin

a collapse. Galaxies, stars, will smash into each other over
and over. Nothing can live through that, on any planet.

You see my concern, all this matter we've got here. Buds
turning into small cups on the branches. Leaves unfurling.

The sheer weight of leaves when before, only branches. All
adding up! I try to lose weight but don't. How many more

electromagnetic waves can be crammed into the air before
the phones grow heavy with language, before language

collapses into noise and we have to hold our ears? Already
it's impossible to carry on a conversation in a restaurant!

But out here it's still so spacious, on top of the earth
where gravity only whispers its name. Don't think I don't

appreciate all this, the fields of tender new grasses,
everything rising and spreading for 200 billion years.

But the sun has only 4.5 billion years before it dies. in 100
billion years the carbon cycle will end, the seas will evaporate.

Everything will go extinct. I think the universe must be
thinking this, also, the way it gives forth all the babies

with their darling noses and delicate fingers and the shutters
opening their wings to a soft breeze and the small red spiders

spindling the corners. To make everything glitter, almost neon, you might say, against the dark. Like a painting on black velvet.

ANIMALS SOLVE PROBLEM OF RUNNING OUT OF PLACES TO LIVE

I
The lined flat-tail gecko is working to solve the problem
of the wall. It needs its own world, not the concrete
one. However, there is only one world, and the lined
flat-tail gecko is the least of its worries. This world
attempting to homogenize to suit the humans.
The gecko thinks to make itself useful. It has cute
little toe pads like spatulas, so it can climb walls.
It climbs inside and eats mosquitoes. It chirps and clicks.
It licks its corneas to keep them clean because
it can't close its eyes. It offers its peculiarities as gifts.
It is willing to be a pet. Look, it says, you can own me,
too, along with your house and everything else.

II
Honduran white bats fit like cotton balls
under a leaf. That is the way we know them, as
metaphors. We also like to say they make leaves
into tent homes. They will nurse each other's young.
So cute. They have lost half their range.
First I wrote rage. Things without rage don't
survive, either. The smaller animals generally don't
feel rage, not our kind, made of a rotten heart.
The bats can store carotenoids under their skin,
which may be a cure for macular degeneration.
They had better make themselves useful. In that way,
everything can work together for the best.

III
People want everything to survive,
but most of all themselves. People still have lots

of places to live, if they keep moving away from
the floods and collapse. The tropical forest
tried to shelter the animals as long as it could,
but you know what happens. The seepage salamander,
the Folohy golden frog, the furry-eared dwarf lemur,
the Grandidiers tufted-tailed rat. I love the names
we've given them as they appear to us and disappear.
We see them and then we don't. There is a vague
feeling of mourning, not for any one thing. It is hard
to know where the sadness might be able to live.

WALK III

When I'm walking, I am totally inside experience.
It flows by me, I break it into waves. I think I want
to write a poem about that, but the idea is so
mundane, made up of only the two parting sides,
observation and reflection, inner and outer, stirred
into a pudding. The two massive trunks of the copper
beech tree across the street have grown together,
their smooth old skin drooping around its knotholes,
top branches lopped off because of disease
or something. What happened to the copper beech
I planted in our dreary subdivision in Delaware, back
when I was married to misery? They last up to
120 years, but their shallow roots make them more
vulnerable to the elements, which then included
paint fumes from the Chrysler plant and no decent
topsoil, mostly clay, the earth having been stripped
for planting houses. The effort to find the tree
on the Google Earth of my past, plus my arthritis,
has slowed down this so-called poem. It likes to act
as if it's simply coming into being on its own along
the way, which is the suspension of disbelief
necessary. You need that, and loss, to make a poem:
something yearning because otherwise how could it
go anywhere? And it needs folds in space, so time
seems to disappear. I notice I'm now headed down
the paved path through the marsh. Near Division,
the homeless have pitched tents in the pines, leaving
a great mass of trash alongside. They can't be blamed
because where are the trash bins? And they are inside
their lives, not pondering the condition of their
surroundings. I take a picture to send to the proper
authorities. The homeless deserve public services,

too. Along the path, also, the milkweed pods have
    sprung their passengers along the lines of chance
and wind which gives me a flash of pleasure, plus
    relief that this small act of replenishment
has happened on its own, without my poem.

DEAD FLIES

Every day, dead flies here and there
on the floor. I step over them, I get them
with a Kleenex. It's spring, still cold,
windows closed, so they must
have hatched in the walls and lived a life
there, before coming out to die.
I suddenly remember they had a life.
They were eggs, they were larvae,
living their wriggling lives! You could see
through them then! What a strange
affair, to first be this, and then utterly
that. To discover the scrub of hair against
hair, to rub together the glistening
papery wings! To be all touch and suck.
To all at once see the wide scope
of seeing, that seemed to have appeared
from nowhere. To know how to mate
without knowing, to just move
into position, not ugly, not beautiful.
To collect viruses and bacteria without
caring who gets sick. To come out here
on the kitchen floor and lay your finished
life at my feet, to be flushed away as if
you never were. Nothing needs to be said
at your passing, but this is my life, and
there is an incompleteness, pinprick holes
in the fabric if I don't at least add you in.

ROBIN

I check on my robin on her nest. I say "my" robin because
we've been keeping an eye on each other. "Be careful," we say
to each other, each meaning something different. You can see
the waste of the world, the thready nest cascading far lower
than necessary, like a dramatic necklace. What now? I get the
binoculars. "Nothing to see here," she says, unmoving yellow
beak tilted up like the prow of a ship. I'm starting to feel the
way I feel when someone looks straight at me for too long
with none of the usual banter. Embarrassed, reminded of my
body's confusion, stuck forever between animal and celestial.
"Keep warming your eggs," I tell my robin. As if otherwise she
wouldn't. I think I've misunderstood everything. It was those
old books on the philosophy of art that said art had to imitate
life. That I had to make sure life doesn't fly away from me in the
process. How humiliating! Where is it going to go? I'm confused
as to how to proceed. I am sitting here as if I were a Greek god
waiting for the right moment to transform the living into some
grand gesture I could take credit for.

WALK IV

Dips in the path are full of spring sogginess, ruined
    leaves pressed to the dirt, almost black as dirt
themselves. There's sun at last, the turning at last,
    but the woods still seem like an old photograph,
colorless trunks of trees like so many masts harbored
    in winter, small ones getting hold of full sun before
the canopy closes down. The poem seems to have
    wandered into the secret growing before there's any
green evidence. It doesn't even want to be a poem
    of walking if it has to shape up, leave randomness
behind, if it has to acknowledge anything but itself:
    its underneath history, its poetic roots, their exact
support, their spreading in perfect relation to the clever
    new things said aloud. The poem zeros in on one
dead tree with very large turkey tail mushrooms
    fanned out on its side like sturdy spaceships. I've tried
grinding them up to make tea. They're good for
    various cancers; they're good for nearly everything,
including the poem. You can only walk so long
    before you start trying to fix the world, or yourself,
or you start thinking of the walk as medicinal,
    or a quest, Dante-esque. It loses its verisimilitude.
I notice the bridge over the little stream has lost its
    top log to ice or rot, and I think, dangerous, but who
will fix it? My shoes are a mess, now, even though
    I step aside onto the dry leaves. And uphill, the very
small rise my arthritis is willing to go for, stones
    are slick. Nothing wants me here, yet. Nothing is
ready to be expansive enough. It is all simply being
    itself, lovely enough for the purpose, if the word
lovely must be applied, to strike some conventional note.

PHOTO OF TWO OLD MEN

One with his bicycle, stopping
for a chat. I think they are Russian,
or French. They are not American
because they are too much at ease
in the world. Their day is only their day.
They are not solving it but leaving it alone
as if it were a stray dog underfoot.
They might be Polish except they are not
that serious. It is cold, cold enough
for gloves and heavy coats. The one
with the bicycle has a large satchel,
its strap wrapped around the handlebars.
He is busy but not that busy.
It makes you glad to be alive, that old men
can stand and laugh. And weep, you think,
at other times. There is a constant mysterious
feeling about old men, how they have
melted down desire and rage to a pudding.
How everything is fine not because of
anything, not because of the wars
and starvation and terrible children,
but because there is this meeting, a nice
surprise. The sweetness of old men
is like a delicate whiff of apples.
The earth has settled into its ridges
and grooves and its trees wait quietly
for spring. The future has been taken up
by the young, who will do everything
wrong, but not wrong enough
to spoil this good conversation.

SOMETHING ABOUT OLD WOMEN

Something about old women, about
how they take care of the old men.
Not about the old women being strong.
More about the way people go on as things
fall apart around them, as they too
fall apart and one by one the witnesses
to their lives die until it seems
nothing sees them. The old men can barely
see, barely hear, but there is the space
around them where they used to be,
the pattern of days, so that is something
to maintain. Out on the street the old men
are walking their tiny dogs.
They are doing what's left to them to do.
The appalling mystery has arrived
in the form of dog walking.
The old women watch to make sure
the old men don't fall. They have given
their all to a failing enterprise. Below
on the wide porches on some evenings
the young women will be photographed
freezing in their sleeveless gowns
and the young men will fling their sport coats
over their shoulders. The women
will be practicing their beauty before it fail,
as John Crowe Ransom said in his poem.
What did we want? It was always
somewhere else. What is it about
old women that hardens and softens
in opposite directions? Hardens to what
must be borne, softens to what must be
looked after, picks up the ends as they loosen,

and makes them into sweaters.
The young men run their Labs, their retrievers,
their German shepherds, while one woman
walks her aging Scottie slower and slower
every morning. There is that feeling
of early morning space around emptiness,
but it is actually full of the old women at home,
alone with everything. They have said yes
to all this. A woman who is almost 100 stands
on her balcony with her accordion
and plays for the people passing. Every day
she wears a tam that matches her clothes.
The house of the body is propped up
as long as necessary. When it begins to
fall away the real house is seen,
no windows and doors to get in the way.
It is like the poet Issa's haiku, the cricket
floating downriver, singing.
When a poem becomes as short as a haiku,
everything can be said. This one is longer
because the old women need
nothing. It is the least I can do.
When hope is not necessary, you can be
generous. You're not so much giving
a poem but singing like the cricket,
not because you're headed hopelessly
downriver, but who's left to sing, if not you?

GRANDDADDY LONG LEGS

Back then there were granddaddy long legs under every log.
Not so many now. The artist Louise Bourgeois made a huge one
for the Guggenheim Museum. It lifts like a spacecraft over the absence
of real ones. I liked to have them crawl on me because they weren't
on me, only the shiver of their tiny feet. I had a box of treasures:
a smooth stick, a white rock, a dead spider curled so tight
it could be dust. Even here children have made a fairy garden
in the woods in the folds of a dead log. Tiny stick table, moss,
tiny mushroom house, tiny white fence. I like how the imagination
turns a person inside out so the mind isn't sure whether
it's in or out. Everywhere, things are in motion and we're made of
everything. So many holes in us, the whole world passes through!
You could say Bourgeois' spider hovers like a mother over her brood.
Maybe that's its appeal. On the other hand, it's kind of a secret fear.
Anything can touch us so lightly we hardly know. We're populated
by so many microbes and flora that we don't exist without them.
As helpless as infants! Ninety percent of our cells are nonhuman.
We're falling apart all the time, leaving flecks of ourselves caught
in the corners. The longing for a hovering mother holds us
a little bit together. The earth is almost a sob of tenderness.

BLACK

So many large blackbirds in the field! The grass was so dry the birds were heavy against it, lifting off only a foot or so and landing splay legged. Against the pale, their beaks pecked and lifted leisurely, my steps apparently not a serious crime. The route was flattened down by use. The heads of the crows curved softly toward their blunt beaks like the tracings of a thumb. Their bodies glistened. There was something about the glistening that was cheering, As if black's absorption of light had refused to go on forever, so turned a little back in this way. A disclosure, a light-river that was also terrifying, the way it teased on the edge of forever. To try to imagine what it would be like to be blind, try to think how it "looks" behind your head. But that isn't it, either.

*

What it is to be black/Black, I have no right to say. I, whose absorption level is so low I am made of reflections. I, who have been slowly fading since the great African diaspora. Who have faded enough not to be a target. More black people live in the U.S. than anywhere else! But not where I live. Since Jamestown, the U.S. has been absorbing. True black people are a glistening ebony. True white people want to turn a little tan, but not get cancer from it. I want to understand black, but black has had enough of my understanding, my facts with their crisp doctor's coat. I have a brick that says, good god, it was made by slaves on my grandmother's family farm. A *Slav*, probably related to *slovo*, "word, speech," which suggests a member of a speech community. My grandmother could not be welcome in that language. I am not welcome. To even talk about not being welcome may be a transgression when the only appropriate response is silence. To transgress is to try to escape in the opposite direction. To break in. Diogenes wrote that it is absurd to bring back a runaway slave. "If a slave can survive without a master," he wrote, "is it not awful to admit that the master cannot live without the slave?"

*

A blackbird only means a black bird. The name was first noted in 1486, applying to this black one, not the raven, rook, carrion crow, or jackdaw. Up to the eighteenth century, "bird" was used only for smaller birds. Larger ones were called "fowl." The blackbird was the only conspicuous black bird in the British Isles. It seems to me my birds' bills were not yellow, but black. Were they blackbirds, then? Was the sun in my eyes? There's a kind of shadowland involved in looking. Once the light rays enter, they are turned upside down, digitalized, fed to the city of the brain with its million lit up signboards. They are making their products look good up there, glossing over the possible flaws. They make people want what they may not be able to afford, what may be bad for them. I would say grackle, but the tail was shorter, and no iridescent colors, only the glistening. The blackbird was first called *ouzel, ousel,* or *wosel.* In *A Midsummer Night's Dream,* Bottom refers to "The Woosell cocke, so blacke of hew, With Orenge-tawny bill." There it is again, the orange I didn't see. They were very black, all black, the ones I saw. I saw because of the contrast. Of course the blind spot in the center of my retina doesn't know it's blind because the brain fills in information.

*

Sometimes it is important to keep silent. Sometimes sunlight is too much release from longing, or from loss. I don't like to talk about it. For instance, that past marriage I think of as a black hole. What good would it do to, to tell it again? To tell it. Would you feel sorry for me? Would I then walk away from the steaming pitchblende, released? And then what? And suppose I apologize for the slavery? The gunshots, the nooses? I am not in a position to answer this question. The shots, the bombs, are making too much noise. The thwanging against the prison bars. To say something happened in the past is a way of making a movie of it. As if I weren't the happening itself and am still happening. You could say I am the secret of myself, overlaid like a shadow on myself as I walk, the sun at high noon. You could say I am haunted.

*

Crow, soot, carbon, charcoal, ants, licorice, shoe polish, ink, space, blackboard, raven, onyx, panther, night sky, tar, asphalt, coal, burnt food, obsidian, ebony, tuxedo, black squirrel, tree trunk against the dawn, loon feather, blackberry, neptunite, black tourmaline, goth fingernails, dragon-eye fish, melanistic jaguar. Halloween mask, boot, cat, crayon, olive, pupil of the eye, bear, swan: maybe, maybe not. (Some information escapes, even from black holes.) Power, elegance, sophistication, status, formality. Evil, death, grief, mourning, the occult. Mystery, bleakness, heaviness, depression, rebellion, fear. Vantablack, made with carbon nanotubes, is the world's darkest material, It absorbs 99.9% of light, making the surface it covers look like a void. Crevice, crevasse. For that matter, darkness is usually the same speed as light.

*

The uninvited thought, the fear, flaps overhead, not exactly hovering. More purposeful, a blackbird looking for a place to land. As if it were a vessel full of police or heat-seeking missiles instead of roaming lazily looking for caterpillars, beetles, worms. As if it were coming straight at me. Though I am not sure it is fear coming at me. It might be love, with its own difficulties, its talons, its serrated edges. Consider the figure in the black sweatshirt, hood pulled up, coming down the sidewalk. It could be St. Francis in his habit or it could be Death. Or it could be a kid sent to the 7-Eleven for cigarettes. The uninvited thought hovers, stirs. It comes from so far off it is my DNA, it is my topography. You could call it an inflammation from the past that once switched on damaging genes, that dysregulated my proteins. The health of the body depends upon a stable childhood, upon love. A potent imbalance can cause disease, animosity, madness, maybe a thousand years later. All I can do is subject myself to a regimen of cure with the medicines available. All I can do after that is hope and pray like a peasant in the field, watching for rain.

III

"The Brain—is wider than the Sky—
For—put them side by side—
The one the other will contain
With ease—and you—beside—"

—Emily Dickinson

EVER-FIXÉD MARK

Alexander Grothendieck (1928–2014)
"The greatest mathematician of the 20th century"
—*Le Monde*

Like the fathoms where leviathans
    keep their universe, play and suckle, feed—
        the mind can do the same—create

entire universes of just one equation! The space
    that fills all directions. A full fifty years
        after Einstein there's Grothendieck—

say GROAT-en-deek—stateless son of revolutionaries,
    father dead in Auschwitz, mother fought
        with anarchists against Franco,

survived as a teenager, dirt poor, picking grapes
    with his mother before she died of TB.
        Father only a string of aliases.

The unpinned mind goes floating off. I wouldn't
    say he dreamed of unifying all mathematics
        to gather his losses. I wouldn't

psychologize. Haven't I wished also to see
    what can't be seen, touch the hem of it,
        "the heart of the heart," as he called it,

that left him babbling incoherently, owl-wide
    eyes? Can you get there with a poem? Where
        is "there"? His professor had said,

see if you can solve one of these fourteen
            unsolved problems for your thesis. He'd solved
                    them all. The mind restless

if it's larger than the given dimension. The mind
            growing fanatical, tracing equations over and
                    over, punching through the page. Until

the room brightens with day, the lamp's kerosene
            gone. Where have you (you) been?

*

Intricate theoretical architectures
around the simplest questions,
zooming farther and farther out,
then focusing sharply, the way
the eyes adjust to distance. Take
a dot—not dimensionless, but
teeming like a fishpond with life.
Not a dot, but a relationship—no
pond without a bank, no bank
without a pond. If you stay
with this like a monk, all day
every day, boundaries fall away
yet still stay sharp as swords.
Explain that. No one dare explain
enlightenment. Heisenberg found
that looking at anything alters it
completely. What is every poem
but a longing. Try to say for what,
and you're stuck talking about love,

itself undefined, abstract, so you
talk about hair and lips, but they're
not it, so you talk about gentleness,
intelligence, but they're not it.

*

All branches of mathematics ought to come together.
        Decartes turned shapes into equations: G called
                what hides behind them a *scheme*,

every equation only a shadow, a projection flashing forth
        "like the contours of a rocky coast illuminated
                at night by the rotating light of a lighthouse."

Sounds like Plato, but this is clearly over my head.
        If you burrow thought inside thought,
                people can't keep up. They turn away.

How lonely. Rilke said don't "let your solitude obscure
        the presence of something within it that wants
                to emerge." Maybe you could go farther

with numbers than with poems. Poems, clinging to
        their metaphors. Plato called mathematics absolute,
                necessary truths. Yet supposedly Einstein

wrote on the blackboard, "Not everything that counts
        can be counted, and not everything that can be
                counted counts." What is it I sense?

Maybe this: "What stimulates me is not ambition
        or the thirst for power. It is the acute perception
                of something immense and yet

very delicate at the same time," said G, pacing
        the classroom: handsome, imposing, athletic,
                square jaw, broad shoulders, corners of his

thick lips turned up, as if mischievously. "My first impression
        upon hearing him lecture," said one professor,
                "was that he had been transported

to our planet from an alien civilization in some distant
        solar system in order to speed up our evolution."
                Not to solve famous problems, but to reach

such an understanding of the measureless deep
        that the solutions would fall out on their own.
                "Like softening a walnut in water," he said,

"so that it can be peeled open like a perfectly
        ripened avocado." What he still hadn't solved
                when he died: he called it *motive*:

a ray of light that illuminates every conceivable incarnation
        of a mathematical concept. Couldn't you as well
                call it the eye of God?

You can only see glimmers. You can posit only so far.
        You have to leave intellect behind.

*

You break down concepts,
remove layer after layer
until there's nothing there,
an apparent vacuum.
I sat for weeks staring
into space, reading trivia.
Was I done, could I not
write poems anymore?
All those thoughts about that.
About what could live
inside that space. I lean in:
hello hello! I follow G
into the cave where thought
fizzles, dark opens its eyes into
the interior, indistinguishable
now from poetry, lifted
in his case entirely away
from the Cartesian plane,
into the bizarre space
of complex numbers.
I don't understand them.
I only know the process of
lifting away, when language
slips out of your hands and
shows you its interior, not
what it means. Beyond that.

*

In the sixties, G taught in Vietnam. Americans later bombed the school and killed two professors and dozens of students. He was a changed man: in one class, he called on students to renounce the "vile and dangerous practice of mathematics" in light of what humanity was facing. Worse than politicians, mathematicians were sleepwalking, he said, toward the apocalypse. He demanded equal time in his lectures to talk about ecology and pacifism. He gave students apples and figs grown in his garden. "The atoms that tore Hiroshima and Nagasaki apart," he said, "were split not by the greasy fingers of a general but by a group of physicists armed with a fistful of equations."

*

He could have been Tolstoy, his house a commune,
              minus superficial adornments. G, ripping
                     out his carpet, making sandals from

recycled tires, pants from burlap, sleeping on the floor
              on a door he had torn from its hinges. Giving
                     everything away, abandoning family,

friends, colleagues. You break down concepts,
              you rescue even the blades of grass between
                     cracks in the pavement. You starve

yourself as close to death as possible. This is how
              you turn concepts into flesh, how you abandon
                     with abandonment: you walk through

now in your sandals. There's a story that he shit
              in a bucket, spread the feces to fertilize
                     his neighbors' farms! He made a cryptic

list, twenty-five items: the stations of his cross: *May 1933*
longing for death; 27–30 December 1933
birth of the wolf; summer (?)

the Gravedigger, and toward the end, *collapse*
of the image, discovery of meditation, prophetic
dreams; nostalgia for God. Is God, then,

what you get when you strip everything away, or
is God a name thrown up as a shield against
the unknowable? In that case, an image

is better, a finger pointing at the moon. Better than
to own the moon, its rough, barren landscape,
dark, then slivering light, then

full blast mirroring your longings. "A perspective
is by nature limited," he wrote. Better to have
many eyes, filling in the blanks.

*

Potato's eyes open in all directions, each a world.
Blesséd be the potato. Blesséd the need to eat, refused.
Blesséd the emptiness, unto death, except for soup
the neighbors bring. Blesséd the dreams:
Le rêveur n'est autre que Dieu.
Blesséd the burning of twenty-five thousand pages
of writing, of the portraits of his father, of his mother's
death mask. Blesséd the elegant blankness
of the page, blesséd the roaming from town to town,
blesséd be invisibility.

At last, G settled at Lasserre, less than an hour
from the concentration camp where his father died,
where he himself almost died as a child, striking out
hungry and barefoot in the cold to kill Hitler.

*

Happy the hours at his piano playing and chanting Mongolian chants.
Happy the seclusion. Burn down the house, even!
Happy the "Declaration of Non-Publication" preventing any of his work
from being read, sold, bought, or disseminated in any way!
Happy, happy, the erasure of a life.

*

The American mathematician Leila Schneps walked town
        to town with a photo of G, of who used to be
                G. No one recognized him. At last she sat

in front of the only organic market in the region.
        Old man, heavily bearded, wearing a monk's habit,
                buying green beans: she knew his eyes.

He escaped, he said, for the protection of mankind.
        He wouldn't say what he meant when he spoke
                of "the shadow of a new horror."

She never saw him again.

*

Love is not love
Which alters when it alteration finds,
Or bends with the remover to remove:
O, no! it is an ever-fixéd mark

Questions:
When the ever-fixéd mark
dissolves, when component parts
dissipate, what is love?
How far is it possible to lean
beyond which sense
makes no sense? Does reason
at last disappear under thought's
fierce microscope? Is what seemed
to be sanity only a freeze-frame
in the randomness?

Answers:
get your sea legs, quit throwing up
over the side. Disappear, or disappear
who you thought you were. Burn
the house, unscrew the locks
from the doors, the doors
from their jambs. Take my very own
heart and give it to the playful whales,
to the gentle clicks and moans
of the mostly unknowable

IV

"Let reason flow like water around a stone, the stone remains."
—Jane Hirschfield

THIS WEEK

Sunday

I need to write something to fasten down the intangible,
just a corner to catch in a seam, the rest fluttering,
the flag of a foreign country. In typing class my fingers
learned how to place themselves on the optimal keys
to reach the rest. I don't have to think, now. It is as if
a little person is in my brain, one who stumbled
out of a bar, slept on a street corner, and finally found
the right door and key. I've been waiting all night
and because of love, am willing to listen to the mumbled
excuses, smell the fumes, and even say yes, you're right,
because I see she's gotten to the bottom of things
but I'm the one who has to take care of her delicate
self, the one who'll tell her in the morning what she said.

Monday

I apologize for my reluctance to begin another week.
People are already cooking macaroni and cheese
for the poor, the poor are standing outside waiting
for the doors to open on the warmth, other people
have suited up their souls and are pressing the buttons
of their remote starters. I apologize for my jeans,
my threadbare aspirations. The Grecian lyre, the old
music, the carnal grace that moves the heart,
the nobility of failure—what have I but my toothbrush,
my neatly made bed? What profiteth it that I am I,
same as yesterday? *The light foot hears you*
and the brightness begins, said Pindar, putting me up
against it, again, this old task without instructions.

Tuesday

My poor Christmas cactus. Would I throw out a plant
that has been nominally faithful, that reluctantly
blooms, but only when forced? Whose trumpets open
with spare promises. Whose nubs of buds are air kisses.
Must all my plants be employee of the month? What
is the morality in this? I know how I am, how I can toss
anything into the compost bin. Where is my black velvet
shirt that began to gap, the plum-colored Hollywood sofa?
All dispersed, dead skin cells, you might say, floating
offshore. Refugees, you might say if you were thinking
how nothing can be tossed out, really, how even the sky
is crowded with dead satellites, and my ex-husband
is living in Florida this very minute, probably laughing.

Wednesday

They designed a new Prius when I wasn't looking.
It is racy with a black smile at the grill and ridiculous
curves, and I do not want it. I wrote to the company.
I said are you out of your mind? Who buys Priuses?
Sensible people, like me. Remember fins? No?
Guess why. The dealer didn't want to sell me one
anyway. They have a low profit margin.
They put a half-asleep old man at the Prius desk.
The oil industry doesn't want me to buy it, either.
I am over the hump of the buying demographic.
I can drive my old car off the ends of the earth for all
anyone cares. The young are removing me from their
sight as if they were the first humans, inventing fire.

Thursday

This day has been like a jar of capers: tiny thoughts,
immature, dark buds pickled by my insistence
on keeping them for further use. Will death reveal
the "hidden meaning?" Will death locate the shiny
object, so to speak, under the tornado's debris?
Everything is going to understand itself little by little.
Oh, not really. Molecules slip around in the old-fashioned
pinball machine, hit by paddles here and there, sink
at last to where they're sorted and lined up to go again.
I will never get used to this. Not either/or. Only And,
And, and And. "Ah, Love, let us be true to one another,"
said Matthew Arnold, "and we are here as on a darkling
plain." Ka-ching! Score ten points for love, anyway.

Friday

I have told the story of my life so many times, it isn't mine
anymore. Today is no exception. As usual, I awoke needing
Post-it Notes on everything, to remind me who I'd said I was.
It was snowing. I wanted to see how much, but snow
kept getting in the way. Even the streetlight had crept back
into the invisible. What if I have a soul, almost tangible,
that needs tending? I wouldn't know what it eats
or anything. Fish on Friday? I suppose because fish are cold-
blooded which is almost fasting, and fasting is what you do
to see if you can give yourself up, even a little, to see
what's left over. It's a lot like watching the pale glow
over there out of the deep and giving it the name you think
it will want when all this confusion has blown over.

Saturday

Today is the day I go to the market for croissants.
The Nine Bean Rows Bakery woman knows I want
spinach-feta. This makes me happier than you might think.
I am only one in the queue at her table, trays piled high,
and yet she knows my heart. Time inhales us in our brief
mutuality. The croissants are folded, some halfway, some
closed. She thinks I like the closed ones. I let her think that
because mutuality has a little slippage. She wears her
stocking cap indoors against the wind that blows in
as more and more people come. It is so cold out there
in the great storms. In here, you might say, is the triumph
of the small: the hollows of sweetness, the risen, the flaked,
heaped in the long hallway of our passing through.

CLOTHESLINE

I am very aware of the limitations. Once I could fly anywhere
as if the wind and I had a deal. This was before I could see the
other end of the line. My mother would hang out the wash.
The sheets smelled like air smells if it slams into something wet
enough times. Perfectly delicious, which makes me wonder why
just breathing doesn't smell like that. If you're at your desk for
hours, air quits smelling at all. When I string up the clothesline
I wrap it three times around one cedar tree and three times
around the other and pull hard, which keeps the small one less
bent for the summer. The line is holding up swimsuits and the
tree. I don't like to see a saggy clothesline. It smacks of sloth.
If you have to have two ends, you should try to make what's in
between have good posture. Maybe I am overly precious about
this, but I want to be vigilant in this job of living. Looking
down the row I want to see clothespins holding things up as
long as it takes.

NIGHTHAWKS

At the airport café, the man with white rubber gloves pulls the
full trash bag out of the bin. He ties it shut and stacks it on his
mound of bags. He stretches a new one over the edge of the
bin and with a small red plastic tool, punches holes around the
edges to keep the bag from blowing up like a balloon as trash
is dumped in. He pushes the curtains back in place under the
coffee bar with the thermoses of skim milk and half & half. He
is contributing to the sanity of the world without giving it much
thought. I wish he would swipe off my table and sweep under it.
There is a late night mess, but I am working around it, keeping
my pizza box to hide the older crumbs, placing my feet carefully.
Some people stay put, some must carry things away. The soldiers
at the next table are quietly talking, while the ones in the
runway glare out the window stand at attention as the casket is
lifted by machine into the cargo hold.

ALL THOSE DEAD TREES

I was driving along 31 North, the patch where the trees are
dead. Acres of them, trunks bare and whitening. I was listening
to opera, I don't know which one. I don't know what killed the
trees. I was driving while the singer was crying for the trees. It
was all soprano: driving though the dead, unbearable. I have
driven this way many times and the trees are still dead. They
have been gray so long, accompanied now by the high notes.
I was traveling along a timeline between here and there. I saw
the trees as wrongness, their delicate remains as wrongness,
and in this I guess I was complicit in trying to tip the universe
to one side when it has been getting along forever swinging
and correcting. The polar ice caps loosening their shoulders for
the long swim. The trees have been doomed to become almost
shadowless among the small cedars. If love gets hopelessly lost
trying to make music of it, I suppose love will have to find
another love. Something will be loved. All I know is that the
shag and dignity of death were accompanied by unknown
opera, unknown singer. And along that part of the road, the
center line had been deliberately roughed up to warn you if you
were half asleep and crossed it. Sometimes you need to cross it a
little in spite of the rumbling. There are so many taut rules, to be
played like violin strings, to get the singing to follow.

THE SCAN

When you have a CT scan, they make you
drink two bottles of cherry water
with barium sulfate in it to reflect your
insides onto a screen to see what's the matter.
Then time elapses while your mind sends
feelers in all directions like string theory,
a number of lives going on in their own
worlds, the one where you live and the one
where you die and all the ones in between
where you are racked with various
disabilities. You will or will not get a call
today informing you which course
you're on. Meanwhile, the others will go
floating weightless, colorless, flexible
as rubber bands into the enormous
landscape. You're familiar with this sadness,
your other selves like sisters or twins
you can't follow, you can't comfort if
they cry. They flash up in your dimension
at the turns, you going one way, heavier,
denser, inside your own self, while
they carry on into the vastness
like silk scarves caught in the wind.

DUCTS

She showed us the picture of hollow ducts, properly lined
with cells. She showed us the ducts full of cancer cells, amok.
I saw how the ducts couldn't breathe. The cancer looked like
an unripe blackberry. Or a raspberry. It helps to move away
from the center of things that way. She ran her hand down my
breasts, one at a time. Just to make sure there was nothing else,
nothing the imaging missed. Each breast like a ski slope, the
sharp rise and then gentle rounding, her fingers like skis. You
want deep snow in case there's a rock or a crevice. The snow will
fill in, or pad the bumps. She showed us the colorful picture
of the ducts on a large laminated sheet with various angles and
magnifications. I was turned inside out. Nothing secret was left
of me. I was fully awake at last, not myself anymore in the old
way of distraction. I was trying to figure out what there was to
save now that I was on the other side of myself.

WALK V

You can take a walk sitting here on your nice brown sofa.
    You can cross the new footbridge on the far end
of Boardman Lake, which ought to be called Ottoway
    Lake, but you know how native names don't count,
as if we intruders invented the lake ourselves. This poem
    is four times removed from reality. Seeing the lake in my
mind is one. The telling is two, the pretending to be there
    is three, your seeing it is four. I haven't done a good job
of describing, yet. The lake is four miles long. I put myself
    at the south end, on the long bridge that crosses where
the swans and ducks live, where it's shallower. Today
    there are wood ducks! There used to be nothing until
the footbridge, because you couldn't get there. At least
    it would seem like nothing to you. Now there's something,
because of the bridge and because of this poem!
    The bridge has bump-outs so you can sit or fish without
being disturbed by walkers or bikers. There are bright
    orange life jackets on posts along the bump-outs.
The lake is clear. Think of that, sitting there on your sofa,
    looking all the way to the bottom! If you were there,
would it be more real? Maybe I need to say more about
    the ripples, and the mute swans. I can put signets in, too.
I think six or seven, still brown and fuzzy. I once saw
    a signet riding on its mother's back. It seemed like a vision
just for me! It wasn't in this lake. I can move to a different
    lake but how would you know unless I tell you?
There may not be signets in Ottoway/Boardman Lake
    at the moment, but what the poem has in mind is giving
you something to work with. I may be wrong about
    the life jackets. They may be scattered along the railing,

but I put them in the bump-outs to give the people
standing there a job to do, if necessary. It doesn't
matter if it's all illusion because it's the life we have, and we
don't want to go around thinking it isn't real, do we?

FUGITIVE DUST

Dust kicked up by vehicles on roads may cause up to 33% of air pollution. Called fugitive dust, it hangs in the air, minutely. The air is full. The earth is always trying to collect it. Under the bed the dust bunnies are so light I can't catch them. In the Dust Bowl, dust could be caught because of the storms of it, filling bowls, covering the tabletop. You couldn't breathe without gathering a mouthful. Grit is not dust. Grit is bigger. When we say a person has grit, we mean they can catch hold. Dust doesn't catch or grind. In that way it is like the soul. You reach for it and a small puff of air moves it out of your reach. You turn the broom on it and it lifts and moves to the corner. People are always trying to have a soul, to be a good soul, but no one knows exactly what that looks like. Really, words are indefinable that way. The air is full of them, polluting reality, but on the other hand, words are like a spring rain that surrounds the fugitive thoughts and slams them against the earth so there can be the planting, the harvesting.

SUBTITLES

I hate it when it's winter in Finland and
the subtitles are in white. Finnish is like spitting
in a friendly way. When the characters are shouting
at each other and shooting guns, you kind of know
why, but you have to interpret the nuances.
You are always left out to some extent.
You want to feel their pain, you really do.
You feel your body for where it might lodge, but
it's stuck in your brain as a thought of pain, or sadness.
By the time the signals reach your gut,
they've become swaddled in your own language,
which has more rounded vowels and travels
into your body, rocking gently as if it were on a nice
night train.
        And it's always snowing in Finland! Everyone
is wearing heavy coats and big hats so that it's hard
to tell who's who. It's barely worth your energy,
but you do want to see how it comes out,
even if you're not sure what's at stake. Clearly
it's a matter of life and death for somebody.
You want to honor that, even if by the end
there is this slight dull headache.

WATER BEAR, PHYLUM TARDIGRADA

After the apocalypse, there will be water bears.
        They can survive radiation, dehydration, freezing
(alive after years in a glacier), boiling heat, vacuum.
        They are so darling under the microscope,
with eight legs, delicate claws! Also called moss piglets,
        they lumber along like chubby-thighed toddlers
though deep-sea sediment and sandy river bottoms.
        They scurry over lichens and moss on land.
They will be lumbering over the ruins of civilization.
        Some varieties have eyes. They look back at you,
unfazed by your behemoth face. You're not alone.
        The creatures you can't see with the naked eye
are keeping life going amid the horrors. There's that.
        And you, midway between water bears and stars,
with your small range of sight, your short life, suppose
        the giant gods are watching, sending news briefs
on your painstaking work. Suppose they're writing
        a textbook. Wouldn't you want to show how
a person lives, caught between, as it were, but sensing
        so much beyond that it's like being suspended?
You could show them how every step is fearful
        but so tender, like walking barefoot on rocks.

SNAPPING TURTLE

The snapping turtle who lives near our dock
        gets bigger every year. He/she is an island
that occasionally rears its head, big as a fist.

He wants to be left alone. Let's say *him*
        because of his thick muscles, his prizefighter
neck. Once when guys were installing the dock,

he came for a visit. They leapt out of the water
        even though I said he was shy, just curious.
I have the fondness of familiarity, he being

our turtle, as if he chose us. As if our traits
        were superior to the neighbors.' It's like when
you look up and a deer is staring you in the face

and neither of you moves. There are so many
        things you want to say. The deer has chosen
you. Its tender nose has sniffed you out, found

you not dangerous for now, sensitive, even.
        You can almost cross the threshold. You can
almost remember when you were a deer,

a turtle, before you got stuck here being only
        you. You want to explain your way back
to when the gods could move in and out of

anything, so you wouldn't know what you were,
        and went on that way: unsurprised,
growing perfectly into the form you've been given.

WILD TURKEYS

The wild turkeys rise so I can't miss them.
Rise from the field at once, I'm going so fast.

The kind of guilt there is no escaping from,
going so fast in this world of slow flapping

creatures who appear to be leisurely but
really carry on purposefully, while I'm willful,

wanton, speeding slightly over the limit
on a country road. What we're like,

humans. Turkeys bombing my windshield.
One turkey in the mirror flaps helplessly

on the road too far back, and what could I do
but put it out of its misery, and how would I

do that, exactly? Would I dig out the tire wrench
which I've never used myself, which I'm not

sure where it is, and pummel the bird
out of its misery? Would I back up and run it

down again to end its disaster quick?
The thought makes me sick. I can feel it die.

I wish I couldn't see the whole thing
in my mind, the actual thing and the fallout.

I love the wild turkeys, and this is what I do.
I go through life doing this. I am a weapon

in an innocent country, the safety off.

WALK VI

You have to hold onto something to write a poem.
        The strange knobby buds, the deep maroon stems
of dogwoods with no leaves yet. Otherwise, you're
        a ghost among the diligent refiguring, among the potholes.
I am fond of potholes because you have to kind of dance
        around them, and no one would think you're dancing.
It all appears practical. This is what the universe wants,
        for the delicious moves to be also practical. Like sex.
Like forsythia. Mary Delaney cut flowers from paper
        and glued them on a black background, so perfectly
they're almost real. This was the eighteenth century.
        Then Molly Peacock wrote a book about this. Then
I wrote this poem. Am writing. You are witness to
        this seemingly useless flowering. This is what I have.
I bring it to you like a fistful of flowers. Somehow
        we got separated at birth. Someone kept saying
our names. We found our arms and legs and thought,
        what have we here? We were presented as a gift
to ourselves. We sucked on our little toes. This morning
        I was trimming my thick toenails and Ollie was chasing
the clippings. You could say my body's still longing to
        catch itself in its mouth, or in the mouth of the darling
kitten, with random black and white spots and a tail
        dipped in ink. Beginning with longing is the way to write
a poem. Grab hold of the red dogwood stem
        and ask which of you is yourself, and how will you
hold on if you stay this small? It is time to open
        your mouth and let what you were chasing get away.

DOCTOR OF THE WORLD

The day before they remove the cancer on my breast, I am obsessed with small things. I am like the doctor of the world. I am struck by the size of the mosquito, the one on the shower wall, for instance, drifting on its long legs, keeping space between its body and the wall, unanchored as I can never be, with my bulges. There are these creatures on the margins, delicate as needles. I also like finding the mushrooms after this hard rain: perfect white, yellow, bright red, mottled orange. I observe that things are so unlike me, so alien. One mushroom floats from the side of a mossy stump like a spaceship. How have I lived in this world so long without being struck dumb? More and more things emerge from their hiddenness. Maybe the earth is showing its face like a last flowering before it is done. Before the waters and the fires take over. The mushrooms are lifting from the earth for a bare few days, saying, "You didn't know what was here, did you?" And the mosquito, living its life on stilts; it has a heart, actually, its blood a clear liquid. The mushroom has no heart, per se, but increases from within itself. The interior can push up between the leaves overnight. It does not know where its borders are until it reaches the end of itself.

PAPER DOLLS

When tabs would tear, we'd depend
on the ones left, dresses aslant.
Little gloves and hats mistaken for scraps

and lost. it was a matter of keeping things
together. Under the clothes were original
clothes, little slips, fancy panties,

camisoles, hiding the absences. The world
was flat except for the shoebox
that made a house, the Kleenex that made

a bed. They were always going to bed
and getting up, they were always
breakfasting with little bowls made of

a thumbprint of clay. We were not preparing
for the real world, we were not capitulating
with premade possibilities,

we were deep into our own selves
where it was all surprising, the wickedness
we allowed, the routines we disrupted,

the various cross-dressings we thought of
with a fierce emotionlessness.
We took them through routines in their

routine clothes, good children we were,
telling their stories ruthlessly,
making them behave, since our own hearts

flew wild against our strange flesh.

THE GRAVES OF MY MOTHER
AND BROTHER

The graves of my mother and brother
lie side by side in the flat middle

of the country where no one we know
lives any more. Didn't she take care

of him all her life? And continues,
silently, while shadows come and go,

and rain, and occasional snow, and
someone regularly mows. What happens

when no one remembers is a question.
When an album is tossed because

the photos fade. Still, it is not nothing
at the gravesite, I think. So much

tenderness must still hang in the air,
it's bound to collect in every small

whirlwind, corralled in the vastness
like a star, its light reaching a million

destinations long after it ceases
being what it used to be.

WALK VII

I go *shinrin-yoku*, forest bathing, my pores taking in
    phytoncides, the trees' natural defense against
disease. I breathe their communal atmosphere. I want
    to belong to them, except not the beeches, snapped
in half from blight. It's spring, pale green little leaves,
    still limp wristed. I take the boardwalk through
the cedars, the wet black earth, the stream with fallen
    branches, all black with muck. You can imagine primitive
life-forms wriggling to light, the common life, then
    the boots stomping across, the fat tire bikes drawing
their deep lines through. What are the crows saying?
    It's hard, being the alien all the time, listening to
the creatures in their foreign language, everything
    going about its business while your mind is just trying
to figure out where to step next. There's spray paint
    on the half-rotten log railings, psychedelic pink
and orange and blue, initials and hearts: people,
    people! the excess! Call it art, I suppose, what
spills over way past necessity. I mean what's it *for*?
    Everything's *for* something—right arm, left arm,
eyes, a perfect system. A spray can is for spraying,
    but isn't this a violation? Which is exactly what
art is, right? breaking through what was thought
    appropriate. I don't want it here, but that's what
critics always say, as they try to hold the line. Still,
    I don't. Want it here, I mean. How can I forest bathe
with this interference? How can the healing molecules
    reach me when my heart is annoyed? Even the large
flat stone is scribbled on. I could write a poem,
    a parable about nature going on anyway. That would
be nice, as if the world were somewhere out there,
    not here. But it's all more serious. The language I'll
never learn sounds like wind, and is always scattering.

YOU THOUGHT YOU COULD MAKE
THINGS BE A CERTAIN WAY

It's not goldenrod that makes you sneeze.
It's the ragweed that hides among it.
Its small green bloom. Nothing is what you think.
Who knows why people want to shoot other people?
You can speculate all day from inside your mind.
You can blame the most flagrant. It's me! It's me!
it shouts suspiciously. It craves notice even
for the bad. The condition of your nose may just be
your inheritance. There was your father,
lying with his head over the edge of the bed, dripping
Neo-Synephrine into each nostril. Every day,
Neo-Synephrine for the terrible losses, the angers.
Goldenrod is good for inflammation, kidney problems,
gout, muscle spasms. The world is rich with its pollen.
It wants to go on propagating. You are living inside
the flying yellow. It colors your skin with grit.
You thought you could make things be
a certain way. You thought one thing was bad and
another good. You ask for a remedy and you get this
ridiculous entanglement, butterflies over all of it.

WALK VIII

Trekking sticks! They've changed my life! My flesh
        no longer presses down on my damaged spine, step
by step, but is floated like a granddaddy long legs over
        the terrain. I am hiking with the old people, which
might be me, through the wildflowers. An excursion
        through trillium, celandine poppies, violets, hairy
Solomon's seal, foamflowers, the whole blooming hillside.
        I am two exclamation points, on their poles!! One
of the old ones needs watching. He wanders ahead
        with another group, not knowing where he is.
One of us reaches down for some brightness and slowly
        falls forward to the ground, bending one of his sticks.
But we persevere! A grandaddy long legs can shed
        a leg if caught, but the leg never grows back. Humans
are like that. My father's doctor gave him a choice:
        die of gangrene or have the leg cut off. I pushed him
in the wheelchair after that, along the paths, through
        the trees, naming trees and plants. He was happy
enough. The names have been plucked out of thin air
        to hold down the blooming and growing and shedding
and dying. But just for a minute! Just long enough
        for a photo, maybe. I miss all the grandaddy long legs
at the cottage which have disappeared along with
        the insects and the skunk that lived under the porch.
When I smell a skunk smell, I grow nostalgic for the dark,
        for crevices with the spiders and grandaddy long legs,
for the bats and flying ants and worms, for the dank
        dirt. I get nostalgic for the little me who wedged under
and climbed over in search of what was hidden.
        It wasn't the names, but the touch. I could have been
blind. I had to get that close, first, before my legs
        got so long that things started to move far away.

BEDTIME

I'll tell you a story. I am on my paddleboard
which, you know, I'm not on anymore because

of balance at my age. I am looking into
the water at the boat named *Zip* sunk there

years ago which is perfectly preserved for
the fish to swim in and out of and sometimes

get caught. There is a sturgeon six feet long,
the oldest native fish in the Great Lakes.

Suddenly it flops up on my paddleboard!
They're not naturally aggressive, so I use him

for ballast. His long nose points the way as if
he had always been a paddleboard himself.

You wonder that I'm not afraid. How there is
room enough for the two of us. You wonder

how he breathes, how I breathe with a six-foot
sturgeon on my board. Where could I be

standing? Well, my children, the time has come
when fish and tale must merge, when momentum

is all, when the password has been spoken
and angels lift us by their shiny ribbons over

the astonishments. Time passes.
This life is the most glorious dream. We see it

inside our eyes, moving across the waters,
backward and forward. I knew Zip Pixler

before the boat, before her drowned son,
before she never wanted to see that boat again.

It lies in the wavery water, not far off the end
of the dock. Its prow could be a giant

sturgeon: necessary, primitive, its back scaled
like a stegosaurus dinosaur. Time means

nothing after all. What hurts, what holds us up,
still lives just barely too far under to reach.

V

"Behold! the body includes and is the meaning, the main concern—and includes and is the Soul."

—Walt Whitman

WALK IX

I was going to be a biologist, but chemistry!
   I was going to be a scholar, but, you know, libraries!
No trees in libraries, no wildflowers, except pressed
     on pages. I was going to be a poet, but pages!
Blank, terrifying. When I forgot the pages, when I
     forgot poet, I could write the poems. Sometimes
pages creep in. I write on them to make them go away.
   When they're gone, I can negotiate the roots
on the path, climb the hill and try to decipher
     the graffiti on the water tank, the fat iridescent letters
so carefully drawn. Striking evidence of the fame
     of being human. I have been remembering a long
time ago, before the fame. I have been remembering
     grit under a rock, roly-poly bugs and the tiny red
worms with no name. Before the poems, when the way
     was uncluttered. The path through these woods
is used and used. And so many poems about trees,
     how can I start over now? Oh, did you think I meant
my fame? That silly illusion. I meant the grit.
     What my fingers felt like, my chewed cuticles,
the way the roly-poly curled as if I were its mother.
   I was waiting for the opening, the tiny legs spread
across my palm. I'd done something right, I'd held still
     long enough for the other world to unfurl. That was
the beginning, when I was not going to be anything.

THE ASTROLOGER

Don't make me warn you of the stars, too. There is too much
else! The water is coming up. The walkway tunnel is already too
wet to walk through. You need boots, and then you will need
waders. You will be waiting for the dove with the olive branch
to let you know there is land left somewhere. You will have
forgotten words like loam or shovel. Who knows if the stars
will even be alive while their light is still arriving? I don't know
what to tell you to do now. Would it be possible to love things
frantically, with so little time left? What would that look like,
you grabbing me, me almost strangling you, kissing your bald
head, your fingers? How would we love the birds frantically,
with their miniature twitches? The nuthatch sees from upside
down, so cares nothing for the stars. She braces the seed in the
bark of a tree and hacks away at it, to get the meat out. She is a
little army, going at it. Sure, the stars have something to do with
this, from a distance, pulling in to themselves and blazing out.
But they're ignoring us as if we were the crazy cousins down the
block who consult the Ouija and get drunk on weekends and
last week blew a hole in the roof with a shotgun, so now what
will they do when it rains?

WALK X

After the others have left the Memorial Day ceremony,
        our 102-year-old neighbor who landed on the beach
at Normandy the year I was born, sits in the too-bright
        sun, hands folded. That's a lot of facts to pack in the opening
of this poem! After you sort it out, he's still sitting there.
        Maybe he's praying. I think his prayers would so easily
penetrate the scrim at his age, they're like two sides
        of an eyeball, the part where the light comes in upside
down and the part that turns it over again deep
        in the forests of the night. Now I'm bringing in Blake
because there's time, since our neighbor's still sitting there
        in this upside-down world. The forests of the night
are coming soon enough. He's a legend, even without me,
        communing with the flags that mark those lost this year.
Lost being a word the living use. How it looks to me,
        afterlife: the poems, the long-lived stories, unspooling
down a shaft of sunlight through the trees. Always trees
        if it's paradise, and moss you can lie on, and ferns.
The sunlight's broken that way, as all things are broken,
        even here, because you wouldn't want an endless
anything. You'd want paths, their surprising turns, and logs
        to climb over where they fell. You'd want the molecules
of you to move out bravely toward heaven knows what,
        never sure if there will be a re-forming at some point
into your dear familiar self, or not. It takes a lot, here
        in the afterlife, to go on, not knowing, but after a while
it must seem natural. All that knowing, all those so-called
        facts, were a way to get along back then. Already,
my neighbor's turning them loose. He's shuffling with his
        walker back to the porch, the long way around—that's
how he is!—bent so far over he's looking at the ground.
        Apparently you can read the path from any angle.

ABOUT THE PERIOD

It was thought that humans could live almost forever, get bigger and stronger.
Recent studies show that they may have reached their maximum size.

In some African countries, people are getting shorter. Climate change,
lack of food, genetics. A cell grows until it can't support itself.

The size of the earth is a limitation. Like a period. You can only love
what's there. What is love but the imagination holding what can't be held?

You can put your arms around her but it is your idea you hold.
When someone dies, your idea begins shifting because there's nothing

to hold it. It carries on until it runs out of fuel. In the closet are photo albums
of people only I recall. I am holding the album in my head. After me,

I don't know where the molecules will go. Consciousness expands and shrinks
like a garden snake in the sun. I can feel myself growing smaller.

I have lost an inch of height, and my memory for simple nouns.
For example, I was trying to think of the word that means not getting it,

not understanding, not dumb exactly but like living in the wrong country,
or the wrong century. Something about dark, the dark ages. Not exactly.

Benighted!. Good grief, where was my mind? Where are the items
that have been stored there? They have sunk into the sludge

at the bottom of the pond. The sludge is where things stop. It gets very still,
like a peat bog. Humans buried in the bog remain so fresh they could have

died yesterday. All around are flickering will-o'-the-wisps made of swamp gas. They were thought to be fairies because it helps to be able to glimpse

what goes on past the end, to see it shine like a welcome.

THE HOODED MERGANSER CURE

Even before I opened my eyes this morning,
      there was a hooded merganser. I don't know why.
            Then I saw it, its snow-white collapsible crest.

Then Ollie scooched up from his nest at the bottom of the bed
      and the merganser flew off. The scrim between
         inside and outside is delicate.

The hooded merganser is sometimes called a frog duck
      because of its long guttural call that can be heard
         a half mile away. That's what I read but have

never heard. They are the only ducks that eat mostly fish.
      Think of what my mind has built now:
         the hood, the snow, the frog, the call, the fish.

I forgot Ollie. He hasn't forgotten me. He plays with my nose.
      Don't you love the name hooded merganser?
         My mind sorted through to find a word

that would start my day happily. That would stand for
      the strangeness, for the web that stretches from
         there to here, gathering its objects.

Even the mouth, bless it, kissing the streamlined sounds.
      Yesterday I was sad, but today I fluff the hood
         and go on into whatever range is still left for me.